SURVIVAL MODE

A MEMOIR OF HOPE, LOVE AND SURVIVAL

THE WORKBOOK

A 7-STEP ACTION PLAN TO HELP YOU...
- BREAK OUT OF SURVIVAL MODE
- SET YOURSELF UP FOR SUCCESS
- CREATE THE LIFE THAT YOU HAVE ALWAYS WANTED!

JONATHAN EDISON M.Ed.

Jonathan Edison

Copyright

Crown Book Publishing
143 Cady Center suite #165
Northville, MI 48167

Survival Mode: A Memoir- The Workbook ©2014 by Jonathan Edward Edison. All rights reserved. No part of this book may be used or reproduced in any manner whatsoever without written permission except in the case of brief quotations embodied in critical articles and reviews. For more information contact Crown Publishing Inc.

Manufactured in the United States of America

13 15 17 19 20 18 16 14

First Perennial paper back edition published 2014

Designed by Kendra Cagle

For information about special discounts for bulk purchases, please contact
Edison Speaks International, 1-972-755-4231 or www.jonathanedison.com

---

The Library of Congress has catalogued the edition of this book as follows: Edison, Jonathan Edward. Survival Mode: a memoir of hope, love and survival/by Jonathan Edison - 1st edition Crown Publishing ed.
p. cm. ISBN 978-1-4951-2472-3 (alk.paper)

1. Jonathan Edison. 2. Memoir-Biography 3. Survivors 4. African American boys 5. Michigan –Biography 6. Edison, Jonathan-Childhood youth 7. Teacher-Memoir 8. Overcoming obstacles-Professional 9. Grandmother's help 10. Detroit youth 11. Afro-American writers-Biography 12. Memoir-African American
Txu 1-904-337

All Scripture quotations are from the Kind James Version of the Bible, public domain.

JONATHAN EDISON

*This workbook is dedicated
to those committed to creating
different results in their lives.*

"WE CANNOT SOLVE OUR PROBLEMS WITH THE SAME
THINKING WE USED WHEN WE CREATED THEM."
-Albert Einstein

"WE MUST BUILD A DIKE OF COURAGE TO
HOLD BACK THE FLOOD OF FEAR."
-Martin Luther King, jr.

ACKNOWLEDGMENTS

I would like to thank Kendra Cagle for all of her hard work and commitment. Kendra really brought this project to life and I am forever grateful for her talent, creativity and flexibility.

A special thanks goes out to all of you who have purchased this book and are beginning the journey toward self-empowerment. I honor you courage, your commitment, and your dedication.

JONATHAN EDISON

JONATHAN EDISON

CONTENTS & CHAPTERS

WELCOME	1
CHAPTER 1 | WHAT IS SURVIVAL MODE?	3
CHAPTER 2 | WHAT IS YOUR STORY?	7
CHAPTER 3 | ARE YOU IN SURVIVAL MODE RIGHT NOW?	11
CHAPTER 4 | STEP 1 Complete a Personal Inventory	13
CHAPTER 5 | STEP 2 Re-Evaluate your Core Values	17
CHAPTER 6 | STEP 3 Set Short Term and Long Term Goals	23
CHAPTER 7 | STEP 4 Practice Visualization Techniques	29
CHAPTER 8 | STEP 5 Make little Shifts	33
CHAPTER 9 | STEP 6 Find a Captain	41
CHAPTER 10 | STEP 7 Activate the Power of I AM in your life	43
CHAPTER 11 | The Final Analysis	45

JONATHAN EDISON

WELCOME

Welcome to...
SURVIVAL MODE WORKBOOK:

7 STEP ACTION PLAN TO HELP YOU....
BREAK OUT OF SURVIVAL MODE, SET YOURSELF UP FOR SUCCESS
AND CREATE THE LIFE THAT YOU WANT!

Thank you for investing the time effort and energy into SURVIVAL MODE: THE WORKBOOK. Our objective is to help you to identify where you are in life and show you how to get to the next level. This learning system is a powerful tool that can transform your life. This system is specifically designed to develop, transform and create new pathways of thinking.

This workbook includes strategies, tools and techniques that will assist you in setting yourself up for success and creating the life that you want…

As you thoughtfully answer the brief questions included in each section, you will be taking an honest self-inventory. As a result, your future "success plan" will come clearly into focus. Soon you'll be well on your way to being more productive, more successful and making every day count!

Congratulations on making this investment in you!

Jonathan Edison, M.Ed.

LET'S GO!

CHAPTER 1
What is SURVIVAL MODE?

You would be surprised to find out that "Survival Mode" is actually a video game term. It describes the level of the game where the player must survive for as long as possible, while the game sends waves of challenges that become more difficult with each subsequent wave. This mode was created and intended to give the game a sudden and definite ending.

Reviewing your life at this moment are you in Survival Mode?
If you answer Yes…Please describe why.

_____
_____
_____
_____
_____
_____
_____
_____
_____
_____
_____
_____
_____
_____
_____
_____
_____
_____

YOUR EMOTIONAL STATE

Please circle how you are feeling right now...and why.
Ex. I am feeling stressed. I am feeling stressed because I'm not sure how to handle this challenge.

- stressed
- anxiety
- worried
- sad
- unhappy
- eager
- optimistic
- challenged
- defeated
- anger
- emotional
- passionate
- fearful
- uncertain
- disgusted
- sorrowful
- surprised
- dejected
- overwhelmed
- shameful
- thankful
- solid

- reliable
- annoyed
- mellow
- jovial
- incapable
- alone
- paralyzed
- tense
- uneasy
- pessimistic
- powerless
- desperate
- bad
- self-critical
- crabby
- abundant
- playful
- embarrassed
- indecisive
- hopeless
- hopeful

(Of course if there is an emotion that you're feeling and you don't see it listed feel free to add it to the list)

1. I am feeling _____
2. I am feeling _____
3. I am feeling _____
4. I am felling _____
5. I am feeling _____
6. I am feeling _____
7. I am feeling _____
8. I am feeling _____
9. I am feeling _____
10. I am feeling _____
11. I am feeling _____
12. I am feeling _____
13. I am feeling _____
14. I am feeling _____
15. I am feeling _____
16. I am feeling _____
17. I am feeling _____
18. I am feeling _____
19. I am feeling _____
20. I am feeling _____
21. I am feeling _____
22. I am feeling _____
23. I am feeling _____
24. I am feeling _____
25. I am feeling _____

CHAPTER 2
What is YOUR STORY?

Dear Friend,
Everyone has a story to tell. **"I'm wondering what is your story?"** Please write your story down. If you need additional room to write, please feel free to write on a separate sheet.

List ten challenges you currently face:*

1. _____
2. _____
3. _____
4. _____
5. _____
6. _____
7. _____
8. _____
9. _____
10. _____

List ten obstacles that you currently have:

1. _____
2. _____
3. _____
4. _____
5. _____
6. _____
7. _____
8. _____
9. _____
10. _____

List ten FEARS that you currently have.

1. _____
2. _____
3. _____
4. _____
5. _____
6. _____
7. _____
8. _____
9. _____
10. _____

CHAPTER 3

Are You in SURVIVAL MODE RIGHT NOW?

Write yourself a letter. Below write a draft of your letter and then write an official letter to your PAST self and mail it to your FUTURE self.

Please be as descriptive, open and honest as possible.

DRAFT 1
Where are you?

_____
_____
_____
_____
_____
_____
_____
_____
_____
_____
_____
_____

Where would you like to be?

___

What activities will it take for you to get there?

___

CHAPTER 4
STEP 1
Complete a *Personal Inventory*

"This is the true joy in life, the being used for a
purpose recognized by yourself as a mighty one"
-George Bernard Shaw

Dear Friend,
In order for you to get started on your road of breaking out of "Survival Mode" one of the most important things that you have to do is recognize your strengths.

ONE
List 25 (or more) strengths that you currently have.

Example:

1. I have great organization skills.
2. I can dunk a 10 ft. rim.
3. I know how to cook.
4. I know how to save money.
5. I have the stamina to drive cross country.

1. _____
2. _____
3. _____
4. _____
5. _____
6. _____
7. _____
8. _____
9. _____
10. _____
11. _____
12. _____
13. _____
14. _____
15. _____
16. _____
17. _____
18. _____
19. _____
20. _____
21. _____
22. _____
23. _____
24. _____
25. _____

TWO
Create a timeline of 25 (or more) high points in your life, when you were AMAZING!

Example:

1. 1987 I earned my first basketball trophy
2. 1989 I landed my first job
3. 1991 I graduated from High School
4. 1993 I enrolled in Community College
5. 1995 I graduated from Community College

1. _____
2. _____
3. _____
4. _____
5. _____
6. _____
7. _____
8. _____
9. _____
10. _____
11. _____
12. _____
13. _____
14. _____
15. _____
16. _____
17. _____
18. _____
19. _____
20. _____
21. _____
22. _____
23. _____
24. _____
25. _____

THREE
Describe 25 (or more) situations or challenges that you have overcome in your past.

1. _____
2. _____
3. _____
4. _____
5. _____
6. _____
7. _____
8. _____
9. _____
10. _____
11. _____
12. _____
13. _____
14. _____
15. _____
16. _____
17. _____
18. _____
19. _____
20. _____
21. _____
22. _____
23. _____
24. _____
25. _____

CHAPTER 5
STEP 2
Re-evaluate Your *Core Values*

> "I stopped living according to my core values. I knew what I
> was doing was wrong but thought only about myself and thought I could
> get away with whatever I wanted to."
> -- *Tiger Woods*

Dear Friend,
Identifying your core values….is a sure-fire way to break out of Survival Mode…

MY PERSONAL VALUE SYSTEM

"Why do I do what I do?"

-Your values are unique to you-They are what you stand for and how you are known. They form an essential part of your personal code of conduct in life, and your character. They typically influence the way you go about your day to day work. You values are vital and powerful guideposts for your choice making process as it relates to your working relationships and focus of effort.

Directions:

ONE
Find your Top 25 Values. What is important to you in life (not what you "should be" or are "expected to be"). If a word is missing you may create one.

TWO
Rank your Top 25 from (1) most important to (25) least important.

THREE
Record your Top 25 on the following page and write down a description of what each one means to you in your own words.

1. _____
2. _____
3. _____
4. _____
5. _____
6. _____
7. _____
8. _____
9. _____
10. _____
11. _____
12. _____
13. _____
14. _____
15. _____
16. _____
17. _____
18. _____
19. _____
20. _____
21. _____
22. _____
23. _____
24. _____
25. _____

CORE VALUE CHOICES

a

Ability
Abundance
Acceptance
Accomplishment
Achievement
Acknowledgement
Adaptability
Adequacy
Adroitness
Adventure
Affection
Affluence
Alertness
Aliveness
Ambition
Amusement
Anticipation
Appreciation
Approachability
Artfulness
Articulacy
Assertiveness
Assurance
Attentiveness
Attractiveness
Audacity
Availability
Awareness
Awe

b

Balance
Beauty
Being-ness
Belongingness
Benevolence
Blissfulness
Boldness
Bravery
Brilliance
Briskness
Buoyancy

c

Calmness
Camaraderie
Candor
Capability
Care
Carefulness
Certainty
Challenge
Charity
Charm
Chastity
Cheerfulness
Clarity
Classy
Cleanliness
Cleverness
Closeness
Cognizance
Comfort
Commitment
Compassion
Competence
Complacency
Completion
Composure
Concentration
Confidence
Conformity
Congruency
Connection
Consciousness
Consistency
Contentment
Continuity
Contribution
Control
Conviction
Conviviality
Coolness
Cooperation
Copiousness
Cordiality
Correctness
Courage
Courtesy
Craftiness
Creativity
Credibility
Cunning
Curiosity

d

Daring
Decisiveness
Decorum
Deepness
Deference
Delicacy
Delight
Dependability
Depth
Desire
Determination
Devotion
Devoutness
Dexterity
Dignity
Diligence
Diplomacy
Direction
Directness
Discernment
Discretion
Discipline
Discovery
Discretion
Diversity
Dreaming
Drive
Duty
Dynamism

e

Eagerness
Economy
Ecstasy
Education
Effectiveness
Efficiency
Elation
Elegance
Empathy
Encouragement
Endurance
Energy
Enjoyment
Enlightenment
Entertainment
Enthusiasm
Exactness
Excellence

Excitement
Exhilaration
Expectancy
Expediency
Experience
Expertise
Exploration
Expressiveness
Extravagance
Extroversion
Exuberance
Evolution

f

Facilitating
Fairness
Faith
Fame
Family
Fascination
Fashion
Fearlessness
Fidelity
Fineness
Finesse
Firmness
Fitness
Flexibility
Flow
Fluency
Fluidity
Focus
Fortitude
Frankness
Freedom
Friendliness
Frugality
Fun

g

Gallantry
Generosity
Gentility
Genuineness
Giving
Grace
Gratefulness
Gratitude
Gregariousness
Growth
Guidance

h

Happiness
Harmony
Health
Heart
Helpfulness
Heroism
Holiness
Honesty
Honor
Hopefulness
Hospitality
Humility
Humor
Hygiene

i

Imagination
Impact
Impartiality
Impeccability
Independence
Industry
Ingenuity
Inquisitiveness
Insightfulness

Inspiration
Instinctiveness
Integrity
Intelligence
Intensity
Intimacy
Intrepidness
Introversion
Intuition
Intuitiveness
Inventiveness

j

Joy
Judiciousness
Justice

k

Keenness
Kindness
Knowledgeableness

l

Lavishness
Leadership
Learning
Liberation
Liberty
Liveliness
Logic
Longevity
Love
Loyalty

m

Majesty
Mastery
Maturity
Meekness

Mellowness
Meticulousness
Mindfulness
Moderation
Modesty
Motivation
Mysteriousness

n

Neatness
Nerve

o

Obedience
Open-mindedness
Openness
Optimism
Opulence
Order
Organization
Originality
Outlandishness
Outrageousness

p

Passion
Peacefulness
Perceptiveness
Perfection
Perseverance
Persistence
Persuasiveness
Philanthropy
Piety
Playfulness
Pleasantness
Pleasure
Plentiful-ness
Poise

Polish
Popularity
Potency
Practicality
Pragmatism
Precision
Preeminence
Preparedness
Presence
Privacy
Proactivity
Proficiency
Professionalism
Prosperity
Prudence
Punctuality
Purity

q
Qualification
Quietness
Quickness

r
Realism
Readiness
Reason
Recognition
Recreation
Refinement
Reflection
Relaxation
Reliability
Resilience
Resolution
Resolve
Resourcefulness
Respect
Restfulness

Restraint
Reverence
Richness
Rigor

s
Sacredness
Sacrifice
Sagacity
Saintliness
Sanguinity
Satisfaction
Security
Self-control
Selflessness
Self-realization
Self-reliance
Sensitivity
Sensuality
Serenity
Service
Sexuality
Sharing
Shrewdness
Significance
Silence
Silliness
Simplicity
Sincerity
Skillfulness
Smartness
Sophistication
Solidarity
Solidity
Solitude
Soundness
Speed
Spirit
Spirituality
Spontaneity

Stability
Stillness
Strength
Structure
Substantiality
Success
Sufficiency
Support
Supremacy
Surprise
Superbness
Supremacy
Sympathy
Synergy

t
Tactfulness
Teamwork
Temperance
Thankfulness
Thoroughness
Thoughtfulness
Thrift
Tidiness
Timeliness
Traditionalism
Tranquility
Transcendence
Trust
Trustworthiness
Truth

u
Understanding
Uniqueness
Usefulness
Utility

v
Valor

Variety
Victory
Vigor
Virtue
Vision
Vitality
Vivacity

w
Warmth
Watchfulness
Wealth
Wholesomeness
Willfulness
Willingness
Winning
Wisdom
Wittiness
Wonder
Worthiness

z
Zeal
Zest
Zing

What does this mean for you?

1. _____
2. _____
3. _____
4. _____
5. _____
6. _____
7. _____
8. _____
9. _____
10. _____
11. _____
12. _____
13. _____
14. _____
15. _____
16. _____
17. _____
18. _____
19. _____
20. _____
21. _____
22. _____
23. _____
24. _____
25. _____

CHAPTER 6
STEP 3
Set *Short Term* and *Long Term Goals*

> "The greater danger for most of us isn't that our
> aim is too high and miss it, but that it
> is too low and we reach it."
> *-- Michelangelo*

Short Term Goal:
A short-term goal is something you want to do soon. Short-term goals can help you make big changes.

A short-term goal is something you want to do in the near future. The near future can mean today, this week, this month, or even this year. A short-term goal is something you want to accomplish soon.

Long Term Goal:
A long-term goal is something you want to do in the future. Long-term goals are important for a successful life.

A long-term goal is something you want to accomplish in the future. Long-term goals require time and planning. They are not something you can do this week or even this year. Long-term goals are usually at least several years away. *Sometimes it takes many steps to complete a long-term goal.

What are your top 10 Short-Term Goals?

1. _____
2. _____
3. _____
4. _____
5. _____
6. _____
7. _____
8. _____
9. _____
10. _____

What are your top 10 Long-Term Goals?

1. _____
2. _____
3. _____
4. _____
5. _____
6. _____
7. _____
8. _____
9. _____
10. _____

For each goal that you identified develop a long-term or short-term plan (strategies and tactics) of accomplishment. Provide a calendar date for the day you will begin pursuing each goal and a calendar date for the expected date of accomplishment. Write down five important reasons why you chose each specific goal. The reasons will serve as a catalyst for you to get going!

For example:

My plan of action for completing my book Survival Mode goal is:

1. Contact an editor by Jan 31, 2014
2. Finish up chapters 13-21 by Feb 28, 2014
3. Finalize the Cover by March 30, 2014
4. Complete the video trailer by April 15, 2014
5. I plan to complete the final draft by June 1, 2014

My top five MUST (S) for completing this goal:

1. I must complete this because: The people that support my work are waiting on this finished project.
2. I must complete this because: I made my Father a promise that I would complete a literary work he would proud of.
3. I must complete this because: I have a lot riding on the success of this project.
4. I must complete this because: I know that my story and my struggles will inspire others to live better and more productive lives.
5. I must complete this because: My kids have been watching me work on it and it's going to be a celebration when it's finally done.

My plan of action for my _____ **goal is:**

My top five MUST (S) for completing this goal:

1. I must complete this because: _____
   _____
   _____

2. I must complete this because: _____
   _____
   _____

3. I must complete this because: _____
   _____
   _____

4. I must complete this because: _____
   _____
   _____

5. I must complete this because: _____
   _____
   _____

CHAPTER 7
STEP 4
Practice *Visualization Techniques*

*"A blind man's world is bounded by is his touch,
an ignorant man's world by the limits of his knowledge,
a great man by the limits of his vision."*
- E. Paul Harvey

VISUALIZATION TECHNIQUE #1 "CREATE A VISION BOARD"

To get started with how to make a vision board, you'll need these supplies:

- **Poster board.** *(Target sells a really nice matte finish board. I highly recommend it.)*
- **A big stack of different magazines.** *(You can get them at libraries, hair salons, dentist offices, the YMCA.)* Make sure you find lots of different types. If you limit your options, you'll lose interest after a while. When I facilitate my live events, I always make sure we have plenty of Oprah, Real Simple, Natural Home, Yoga Journal, Dwell, Ode, Parenting, Money, Robb Report, and an assortment of nature magazines.
- **Glue.** Not Elmers. *(It makes the pages ripple.)*

Before you begin your vision board:
No matter which method you're choosing, making a vision board that is right for you should be started with a little ritual. Sit quietly and set the intent. With lots of kindness and openness, ask yourself what it is you want. Maybe one word will be the answer. Maybe images will come into your head. Just take a moment to be with that. This process makes it a deeper experience. It gives a chance for your ego to step aside just a little, so that you can more clearly create your vision.

Put on soft music. My favorite music for activities like this is Anugama Shamanic Dream I and Shamanic Dream II. I love these CD's for massage or any activity where you want to keep your mind quiet.

How to make a vision board in 5 steps:

STEP 1:
Go through your magazines and tear the images from them. No gluing yet! Just let yourself have lots of fun looking through magazines and pulling out pictures or words or headlines that strike your fancy. Have fun with it. Make a big pile of images and phrases and words.

STEP 2:
Go through the images and begin to lay your favorites on the board. Eliminate any images that no longer feel right. This step is where your intuition comes in. As you lay the pictures on the board, you'll get a sense how the board should be laid out. For instance, you might assign a theme to each corner of the board. Health, Job, Spirituality, Relationships, for instance. Or it may just be that the images want to go all over the place. Or you might want to fold the board into a book that tells a story. At my retreats, I've seen women come up with wildly creative ways to present a vision board.

STEP 3:
Glue everything onto the board. Add writing if you like. You can paint on it, or write words with markers.

STEP 4:
(optional, but powerful) Leave space in the very center of the vision board for a fantastic photo of yourself where you look radiant and happy. Paste yourself in the center of your board.

STEP 5:
Hang your vision board in a place where you will see it often.

Three Types of Vision Boards:

1. THE "I KNOW EXACTLY WHAT I WANT" VISION BOARD

Do this vision board if:

- You're very clear about your desires.
- You want to change your environment or surroundings.
- There is a specific thing you want to manifest in your life. *(i.e. a new home, or starting a business.)*

How to make a vision board if you know what you want:

With your clear desire in mind, set out looking for the exact pictures which portray your vision. If you want a house by the water, then get out the Dwell magazine and start there. If you want to start your own business, find images that capture that idea for you. If you want to learn guitar, then find that picture.

2. THE "OPENING AND ALLOWING" VISION BOARD

Do this vision board if:

- You're not sure what exactly you want
- You've been in a period of depression or grief
- You have a vision of what you want, but are uncertain about it in some way.
- You know you want change but don't know how it's possible.

How to make a vision board if you're not quite sure what you want:

Go through each magazine. Tear out images that delight you. Don't ask why. Just keep going through the magazines. If it's a picture of a teddy bear that makes you smile, then pull it out. If it's a cottage in a misty countryside, then rip it out. Just have fun and be open to whatever calls to you. Then, as you go through Step 2 above, hold that same openness, but ask yourself what this picture might mean. What is it telling you about you? Does it mean you need to take more naps? Does it mean you want to get a dog, or stop hanging out with a particular person who drains you? Most likely you'll know the answer. If you don't, but you still love the image, then put it on your vision board anyway. It will have an answer for you soon enough. Some women at my retreats had NO idea what their board was about, and it wasn't until two months later that they understood. The Opening and Allowing Vision Board can be a powerful guide for you. I like it better than the first model because sometimes our egos think they know what we want, and lots of times those desires aren't in alignment with who we really are. This goes deeper than just getting what you want. It can speak to you and teach you a little bit about yourself and your passion.

3. THE "THEME" VISION BOARD

Do this vision board if:

- It's your birthday or New Years Eve or some significant event that starts a new cycle.
- If you are working with one particular area of your life. For instance, Work & Career.

How to make a vision board for a theme:

The only difference between this vision board and the others is that this one has clear parameters and intent. Before you begin the vision board, take a moment to hold the intent and the theme in mind. When you choose pictures, they will be in alignment with the theme. You can do the Theme Vision Board on smaller pages, like a page in your journal.

Some things to remember about vision boards:

You can use a combination of all three types of vision boards as you create. Sometimes you might start out doing one kind, and then your intuition takes over and shifts into a whole different mode. That's called creativity. It doesn't matter how you make a vision board. Once the creativity is there, just roll with it.

Your vision board might change as you are making it. I was just talking with a friend of mine who said that she had been making a vision board for the new year. The theme was all about what she wanted in this year. Then, as she pulled pictures and began to lay them out, the theme changed into a simpler one about her everyday life and the moments in each day. It surprised and delighted her to experience that evolution. You might find that you have little epiphanies from making a vision board.

VISUALIZATION TECHNIQUE #2

Make a Vision Journal

Another option is to use these same principles in a big sketch book. Get a large sketch book and keep an on-going vision journal. This is especially effective if you're going through many transitions in your life.

CHAPTER 8
STEP 5
Make *Little Shifts*

"Change happens when you make changes little by little"
- Jonathan Edison

Little shifts in life allow us to change over time. We all have areas in our lives that need to be shifted to achieve different results.

What are yours?   Come on be HONEST!

Example:

I need to shift my attitude
I need to shift my way of thinking
I need to shift my tardiness
I need to shift my awareness

ACTIVITY #1

1. I need to shift my_____
2. I need to shift my_____
3. I need to shift my_____
4. I need to shift my_____
5. I need to shift my_____
6. I need to shift my_____
7. I need to shift my_____
8. I need to shift my_____
9. I need to shift my_____
10. I need to shift my_____
11. I need to shift my_____
12. I need to shift my_____
13. I need to shift my_____
14. I need to shift my_____
15. I need to shift my_____
16. I need to shift my_____
17. I need to shift my_____
18. I need to shift my_____
19. I need to shift my_____
20. I need to shift my_____

ACTIVITY #2

Describe how you plan to make the little shift.

1. _____

2. _____

3. _____

4. _____

5. _____

6. _____

7. _____

8. _____

9. _____

10. _____
_____

11. _____
_____

12. _____
_____

13. _____
_____

14. _____
_____

15. _____
_____

16. _____
_____

17. _____
_____

18. _____
_____

19. _____
_____

20. _____
_____

ACTIVITY #3

I love myself because...

*For this activity you are going to need a mirror. It can be mounted to a wall or hand held. This little shift is going to shift how you see, feel about and acknowledge yourself. It will also increase your self-esteem and your self-worth.

> "People are like stained-glass windows. They sparkle and shine when the sun is out, but when the darkness sets in their true beauty is revealed only if there is light from within.
> -Elisabeth Kubler-Ross

Instructions:

I want you to stand in front of the mirror and make eye contact with yourself and repeat…..I love myself because fill in the blank 25 times consecutively without pausing and without breaking eye contact. If you break eye contact or pause more than 5 seconds please start over from your first reason.

Example:

1. I love myself because……I am a good father.
2. I love myself because…..I stopped overspending.
3. I love myself because…..I care about people.
4. I love myself because…..I know that GOD loves me.
5. I love myself because……I'm willing to work hard.

What are the 25 reasons why you love yourself?

1. I love myself because… _____
2. I love myself because… _____
3. I love myself because… _____
4. I love myself because… _____
5. I love myself because… _____

6. I love myself because… _____
7. I love myself because… _____
8. I love myself because… _____
9. I love myself because… _____
10. I love myself because… _____

11. I love myself because… _____
12. I love myself because… _____
13. I love myself because… _____
14. I love myself because… _____
15. I love myself because… _____

16. I love myself because… _____
17. I love myself because… _____
18. I love myself because… _____
19. I love myself because… _____
20. I love myself because… _____

21. I love myself because… _____

22. I love myself because… _____

23. I love myself because… _____

24. I love myself because… _____

25. I love myself because… _____

CHAPTER 9
STEP 6
Find a *Captain*

"Make it your business to work with someone who has been there done that and has the T-Shirt."
- *Jonathan Edison*

Dear Friend,

In life I have found that if you want to grow you have to be willing to take on a new perspective. A fresh new perspective can give you the fuel that you need to obtain different results in your life. I suggest that you find a "Captain" to show you how to be a captain. Now finding a captain isn't easy, but it's necessary. Below you will find a list of activities required for you to connect with a "Captain".

Note:
Your choice of a Captain should be based upon where you see yourself. Doing more, being more, accomplishing more.

ACTIVITY #1

Make a list of 25 possible Captains that you would like to connect with.

1. _____
2. _____
3. _____
4. _____
5. _____
6. _____
7. _____
8. _____
9. _____
10. _____
11. _____
12. _____
13. _____
14. _____
15. _____
16. _____
17. _____
18. _____
19. _____
20. _____
21. _____
22. _____
23. _____
24. _____
25. _____

CHAPTER 10
STEP 7
Activate the *Power of I AM* in your Life

*"And God said unto Moses, I AM THAT I AM: and he said,
Thus shalt thou say unto the children of Israel, I AM hath sent me unto you."*
- Exodus 3:14

THE POWER OF I AM

Dear Friend,

I want you to evaluate where you are and what words that you use on a consistent basis. The way in which we describe ourselves is very important as it relates to activating our POWER! Research shows that the average human being speaks at a rate of 150 words per minute and thinks at a rate of 800 words per minute. Further research suggests that the average human being is awake an average of 16 hours a day. This means that a maximum of 144,000 words can be spoken by an individual on a given day. This also means that a maximum of 768,000 words can be thought by an individual on a given day. In total, words spoken and thought by an individual can equal 912,000. That's a lot of words. To begin to better monitor our spoken words and thoughts, let us take the following action steps:

The ability to recognize our feelings as they quickly come over us is called self-awareness, and it is critical to our development in a highly mobile, fast changing, and complex society. Self-awareness is very important.

What you tell yourself is EXTREMELY IMPORTANT! On the next page, make a list of I AM statements to describe a powerful, confident and self-assured you.

Example:

1. I AM Powerful
2. I AM Energetic
3. I AM Going places
4. I AM Smart
5. I AM Beautiful

1. I AM _____
2. I AM _____
3. I AM _____
4. I AM _____
5. I AM _____
6. I AM _____
7. I AM _____
8. I AM _____
9. I AM _____
10. I AM _____
11. I AM _____
12. I AM _____
13. I AM _____
14. I AM _____
15. I AM _____
16. I AM _____
17. I AM _____
18. I AM _____
19. I AM _____
20. I AM _____
21. I AM _____
22. I AM _____
23. I AM _____
24. I AM _____
25. I AM _____
26. I AM _____
27. I AM _____
28. I AM _____
29. I AM _____
30. I AM _____
31. I AM _____
32. I AM _____
33. I AM _____
34. I AM _____
35. I AM _____
36. I AM _____
37. I AM _____
38. I AM _____
39. I AM _____
40. I AM _____
41. I AM _____
42. I AM _____
43. I AM _____
44. I AM _____
45. I AM _____
46. I AM _____
47. I AM _____
48. I AM _____
49. I AM _____
50. I AM _____

CHAPTER 11
The Final ANALYSIS

People are often unreasonable, irrational, and self-centered.
Forgive them anyway.

If you are kind, people may accuse you of selfish, ulterior motives.
Be kind anyway.

If you are successful, you will win some unfaithful friends and some genuine enemies.
Succeed anyway.

If you are honest and sincere people may deceive you.
Be honest and sincere anyway.

What you spend years creating, others could destroy overnight.
Create anyway.

If you find serenity and happiness, some may be jealous.
Be happy anyway.

The good you do today, will often be forgotten.
Do good anyway.

Give the best you have, and it will never be enough.
Give your best anyway.

In the final analysis, it is between you and God.
It was never between you and them anyway.

To find yourself outside or on the other side of Survival Mode one of the most crucial things that you're going to have to do is to make sure that you LOVE YOURSELF. Your self-identity and your self esteem for your life is also driven by what goes on within you. Therefore, it is imperative that you not only work hard for your freedom, but you love yourself in the process…

REMEMBER!

"People are like stained-glass window. They sparkle and shine when the sun is out, but when the darkness sets in their true beauty is revealed only if there is light from within."

-Elisabeth Kubler-Ross

List 50 Reasons why you love yourself:

After you list the 50 reasons why you love yourself I want you to repeat this list to yourself in the mirror looking directly at yourself eye ball to eye ball. Try your best not to break eye contact with yourself and see how far you can go…

Example:

Jonathan…
1. I love myself because: I am a GREAT FATHER.
2. I love myself because: I have a giving heart.
3. I love myself because: I treat people of all types with respect.
4. I love myself because: I'm kind and generous.
5. I love myself because: I give 200 percent to completing my projects.

30 DAY CHALLENGE

For thirty consecutive days you are going to be an ACTIVE PARTICIPANT in creating the life that YOU WANT! This is going to happen through your actions, your attitude, your choices and your consciousness.

In the description section: Layout your goals for the day.

In the event sections: List what actions you are going to take.

You CHOOSE to Feel: This section is up to you… but HOPEFULLY it's positive.

DAY 1

Description #1: _____

Event(s): _____

Description #2: _____

Event(s): _____

Description #3: _____

Event(s): _____

I choose to feel: _____

DAY 2

Description #1: _____

Event(s): _____

Description #2: _____

Event(s): _____

Description #3: _____

Event(s): _____

I choose to feel: _____

DAY 3

Description #1: _____

Event(s): _____

Description #2: _____

Event(s): _____

Description #3: _____

Event(s): _____

I choose to feel: _____

DAY 4

Description #1: _____

Event(s): _____

Description #2: _____

Event(s): _____

Description #3: _____

Event(s): _____

I choose to feel: _____

DAY 5

Description #1: _____

Event(s): _____

Description #2: _____

Event(s): _____

Description #3: _____

Event(s): _____

I choose to feel: _____

DAY 6

Description #1: _____

Event(s): _____

Description #2: _____

Event(s): _____

Description #3: _____

Event(s): _____

I choose to feel: _____

DAY 7

Description #1: _____

Event(s): _____

Description #2: _____

Event(s): _____

Description #3: _____

Event(s): _____

I choose to feel: _____

DAY 8

Description #1: _____

Event(s): _____

Description #2: _____

Event(s): _____

Description #3: _____

Event(s): _____

I choose to feel: _____

DAY 9

Description #1: _____

Event(s): _____

Description #2: _____

Event(s): _____

Description #3: _____

Event(s): _____

I choose to feel: _____

DAY 10

Description #1: _____

Event(s): _____

Description #2: _____

Event(s): _____

Description #3: _____

Event(s): _____

I choose to feel: _____

DAY 11

Description #1: _____

Event(s): _____

Description #2: _____

Event(s): _____

Description #3: _____

Event(s): _____

I choose to feel: _____

DAY 12

Description #1: _____

Event(s): _____

Description #2: _____

Event(s): _____

Description #3: _____

Event(s): _____

I choose to feel: _____

DAY 13

Description #1: _____

Event(s): _____

Description #2: _____

Event(s): _____

Description #3: _____

Event(s): _____

I choose to feel: _____

DAY 14

Description #1: _____

Event(s): _____

Description #2: _____

Event(s): _____

Description #3: _____

Event(s): _____

I choose to feel: _____

DAY 15

Description #1: _____

Event(s): _____

Description #2: _____

Event(s): _____

Description #3: _____

Event(s): _____

I choose to feel: _____

DAY 16

Description #1: _____

Event(s): _____

Description #2: _____

Event(s): _____

Description #3: _____

Event(s): _____

I choose to feel: _____

DAY 17

Description #1: _____

Event(s): _____

Description #2: _____

Event(s): _____

Description #3: _____

Event(s): _____

I choose to feel: _____

DAY 18

Description #1: _____

Event(s): _____

Description #2: _____

Event(s): _____

Description #3: _____

Event(s): _____

I choose to feel: _____

DAY 19

Description #1: _____

Event(s): _____

Description #2: _____

Event(s): _____

Description #3: _____

Event(s): _____

I choose to feel: _____

DAY 20

Description #1: _____

Event(s): _____

Description #2: _____

Event(s): _____

Description #3: _____

Event(s): _____

I choose to feel: _____

DAY 21

Description #1: _____

Event(s): _____

Description #2: _____

Event(s): _____

Description #3: _____

Event(s): _____

I choose to feel: _____

DAY 22

Description #1: _____

Event(s): _____

Description #2: _____

Event(s): _____

Description #3: _____

Event(s): _____

I choose to feel: _____

DAY 23

Description #1: _____

Event(s): _____

Description #2: _____

Event(s): _____

Description #3: _____

Event(s): _____

I choose to feel: _____

DAY 24

Description #1: _____

Event(s): _____

Description #2: _____

Event(s): _____

Description #3: _____

Event(s): _____

I choose to feel: _____

DAY 25

Description #1: _____

Event(s): _____

Description #2: _____

Event(s): _____

Description #3: _____

Event(s): _____

I choose to feel: _____

DAY 26

Description #1: _____

Event(s): _____

Description #2: _____

Event(s): _____

Description #3: _____

Event(s): _____

I choose to feel: _____

DAY 27

Description #1: _____

Event(s): _____

Description #2: _____

Event(s): _____

Description #3: _____

Event(s): _____

I choose to feel: _____

DAY 28

Description #1: _____

Event(s): _____

Description #2: _____

Event(s): _____

Description #3: _____

Event(s): _____

I choose to feel: _____

DAY 29

Description #1: _____

Event(s): _____

Description #2: _____

Event(s): _____

Description #3: _____

Event(s): _____

I choose to feel: _____

DAY 30

Description #1: _____

Event(s): _____

Description #2: _____

Event(s): _____

Description #3: _____

Event(s): _____

I choose to feel: _____

In the Final Analysis what have you discovered about yourself?

Please answer the following questions.

How do you feel after completing the Survival Mode Workbook? Please explain.

_____
_____
_____
_____

_____
_____
_____
_____

_____
_____
_____

_____
_____
_____

Are you still in Survival Mode? Please explain

What do you plan to do differently now that you have completed the workbook?

FINAL THOUGHT

GOD LOVES YOU
and no matter what you've heard or what you've believed in the past...
YOU ARE NEVER ALONE!

CONGRATULATIONS
ON COMPLETING THIS JOURNEY!

Your friend,
Jonathan Edison, M.Ed